Book One: A jar for the jarring
Candice Louisa Daquin

Copyright © 2016 by Candice Louisa Daquin.
All rights reserved. This book or any portion thereof may not be reproduced or used in any manner whatsoever without the express written permission of the publisher except for the use of brief quotations in a book review.

Printed in the United States of America

First Printing, 2014
Originally published by STPG Press, TX USA
79 pages

ISBN 978-1-365-01537-3

Second Edition published by TheFeatheredSleep Press

Library of congress data
A jar for the jarring
Daquin, Louisa Candice
Poetry, 2014

TABLE OF CONTENTS

Nightshade	5
You were young	6
Homemade	7
Grief/Leaf	8
Like that	9
Bluelids	10
Cobweb	11
Small hands	12
One year too long	13
Dart	14
Nothing Near	15
Middle-hardship	16
From the beginning	17
Glowing ember	19
Tenderheart	20
Verbi	21
Gypsy	22
The Corn-maker	23
Hedgerows	25
The mirror and the sea serpent	26
Weave	27
You told me	28
In about 45 minutes I'm gone (or ode to leaving a job)	29
You	30
Imitation of life	31
Desert	32
Manger of constellations	33
Everglades	35
Damask	36
Just a little treacle	39
Drowning in Tenerife	40
The Deity	41
Therapist #2	43

Memory	44
Fame	46
Mine	47
Relation	49
A little death	50
Cheese Plate	51
Lint	52
Coins for a funeral	53
Part Deux	54
Similarity	55
Hazel Eyed Sex	56
All Things	57
Sweet Static Silence	58
Goodbye & Hello	59
Tigers Not Daughters	60
Today's Observation	61
Chick-a-Flicker	62
The night I turned 16	64
The copper wedding dress	65
Pursuing Different Tracks	67
A Jar for the jarring	68
Infidelity	69
Send me with you	70
Merry-Go-Round	71
Lark	72
I want with you to go	73
Who leaves behind	74
Red felt	75
Were I born and you not	76
Clay	77
Hear the Steps	78
Destiny	79

Nightshade

I am no longer the color of nightshade
the color of nightshade is me

in deep water you can see us talking
in silhouette we climb and fall like birds without beaks
tapping in parody, slipping, urgent wet eels

an easy dialogue when behind glass you mouth
words in air you could not speak out loud

You were young

Out of the wrinkle climbs
of a hemmed dress drops
that frugal stitch that binds Truth's cloth

to pay for this weary daydream haloed in leaves
a rope ever tightening or a kiss ever deepening

the fork in the road chooses
as chalk hardens in sun
and children stop being fat and young

as yellow can be silver at night
it takes you down to that green tree

where memory plays on her own
until the needle, ever fragile, is held
between your fingers

steady carved names that stay
after we are gone

Homemade

Quietly
mice roosting in the eaves
dark as buttered moonshine
there is always music, there is always night
cloaking reality & shading the tempers with hush

my feet are long like trails of milk in twilight
shadows echoing off walls in quiet formation
sylphs dress for ballet in the wild with ragged dresses
their hair blood red & damp with excitement

all that was, has been seated & tucked away
leaving a stage glistening & slippery for vice
outside is a step away, a lifetime far
because I am safe here in my homemade jar

Grief/Leaf

You are but a filament
left long in the sun
turning indecipherable
turning golden like leaves.

That autumn I buried my faith
and left it to take root
hoping I could return when ready
and eat the green shoots

Like that

Where in all of this, the day-trips, the postponed hysteria,
the meal at eight, the cat's siesta, the sound of pen on paper,
the consternation on the face of a teacher, the rustle of linen in the dark,
the bird feathers in my throat, the cough medicine turning 3 colors,
the bare feet with chinks for each pair of shoes, the lopsided make-shifts, the tin desk
with nothing noted, the sticky postcards, the surprise guest, the flat tire,
the deckchair facing west, the quiet place,
the unfinished novel, the ink in my eyes, the sound of crickets after dusk,
the television bulb, the sneeze that startles, the bathrobe with rust,
the second-hand ironing board, the beehive in the field, the water filter,
the limeade from sonic, the hanging bird bath, the jar half full,
the picture of my family, the apron string that's torn,
the calendar with a red circle, the day I find out

Bluelids

Violet time, fairy tales, old bound books, balconies with hooks,
swinging plant, midnight chant, hopeful star, rushing car. sofa-ridden,
daytime trivial, unfaithful hour, wilting flower.
watching baby, maybe, maybe, she sleeps like a doll, make-up still on.
bluelids, my own abyss, the bottom of the well, where water remains cold and still.
staring up to the sky, wondering how far, how high, whether warm sun or cold brick,
the tick, tock, tick, a high tea, a simple life, the wet clay of my own face,
the textbook with words erased, the broken shadows, and folded thoughts,
the crushed lilies in my grandmother's drawer, don't open the window,
don't let the world in, let the dust settle now, let us wait a little longer, for something.

Cobweb

When you said I took your trust
and crushed it underfoot
told you things that weren't true
and with lighthearted intention
drove the knife into you.

What you forgot to mention
were the words I leave
like cobwebs now
invisible in light
glittering to recall
but not yet bright
and if we're not careful
they catch in our hair
and we never really know
they had even been there

Small hands

Shoot the moon
and the violet smell
lingering in my palm
crush beneath me
your small hands
the child that didn't grow
whose heart was melted and turned
like pennies into gold
and then when it was dark
tarnished and lost
put somewhere too high
for any of us

One year too long

At this time of year the melon sellers park
and try to hawk by the dirt road
where red mixes with brown and turns golden
water from the summer rain stagnates
and in the air a smell of fern and strange yellow
winding the path to these hollows

I did not lie in the tall grass with you
or dive in green water to catch the silver fish
I did not eat chocolate in front of the TV
or wash myself by the early morning light
where my body would, angular, lean
tired and waiting for sleep again

These things we didn't share or cultivate
time froze and we ran
everything behind us in Technicolor
everything in front blurred
our backs to the world we ran
talking faster than we could understand
so many words and in the night
touching deeper
it felt true then
with the sun coming up
first flowers and trees bloom
no more do you call me
no more do you think on me
but for scorn and regret, a story after wine

or another time, never quite recalled
the bitter taste I left, like wine saved in a cellar
just one year too long, turning from precious
to rotten

Dart

The red dart stuck in wood
leant up against the house we bought
shelter for all the falling down
things I should have known
piercing the wood deeply
I pulled up weeds and wondered
who threw it there and when?
what were they thinking?
leaving it red against the rest
colors we remember in our heart
like my own loss of conscience
dropping it into water and seeing
the ripples peal away from me
I hadn't wanted to hurt anyone
least those I protected
but that's what happened
when I pierced your heart and mine
with the intensity that was bound
to shake everything until almost broken
falling away like shards of glass
what can be done after destruction
when my decisions were the catalyst?

I knew myself not at all
had I looked more carefully
perhaps I would have seen who chose that spot
who lifted their hand catching the sun
and let the dart find its mark
penetrating, a bright reminder
we are not safe, least safe from our own
selves

Nothing Near

There is nothing near
everything stands off
glittering in the horizon
like mirage for the thirsty
I am thirsty
when we talk until 3am
when I clutch the toilet bowl heaving
when I wonder at the chain
that leads us from this point
to the next
and I wonder if you will live
if in ten years
on a full moon like tonight
you'll remember and know
your version of me
never the truth
because that's out in the desert
where my eyes are
staring into darkness
hearing the murmur of animals
walking barefoot among snakes
I am sleepwalking
looking for silver pieces
looking for something I've lost
by my own choices

Middle-hardship

When was your moment?
curled like an 'O' in your mother,
against her heart so stable,
your thoughts so fragile,
was it then?

And as a baby,
sleeping in your liquid body,
finding your kicks and your cries

Before the next,
the newest born unfurls his fingers,
and lays clasp on your mother's heart,
leaving you to take your place,
the middle child

From the beginning

Not sure where to put my next step,
or how to make sure the movement is mine
and not some forgotten hand tail of a daydream,
left-over from all the hope and the times,
I have wished to see your face again,
and know that with your warm breath,
you are there with me once more

Whether it makes sense in this world or another,
there have been times when nothing,
except the thought of you,
has stirred my loneliness and given me
through the maddening silence that followed,
a figure to chase out into the light

And now, there in the frigid moon,
you stand.
your face is bathed in the colors of sunrise,
and your fingers are separated each one,
as if by strength that tugs me closer
and spins our hearts above us,
the dizzying moment in the light,
with rain beginning to fall and
my own words lost in the second before,
I realized what this meant

If you knew, if you could just see into me,
the shards of broken expectations,
hanging from once used swings
dangling useless and derelict,
in my playground of dreams

Persisting, you exist, your mouth is warm,
your kisses intermixed with our tears,

your hands strong and closed about me
as if this moment had been picked from a year,
a lifetime before, and yet so honest and familiar,
deceiving me in my own human weakness,

I must accept you have returned,
I must believe what you have said all along

Glowing ember

They talked about:
working out
revision
working out
revision
I talked about:
Isis
The meaning of circles
Where you could get a good coffee.
We shuffled back to the classroom,
too many neon lights, too many glowing faces,
I longed for darkness and soon I got it,
driving back in the night
I wanted to be cheerful but I couldn't muster a smile,
the tears came out hidden in my hair and the moonless sky,
I would have stood up on my table and screamed,
but my shoes were too dirty

Tenderheart

I wore this color, I think it suits me,
the exact shade of something
I am feeling for you

It could be the season,
but last night I spent
at least 3 hours shopping

If I pick something out
and turn it to see for bruises,
will I catch a flaw?

In my basket, limes by the dozen,
their green skins brushing,
the oil left on my hands

And tonight, through the sheets,
gently, you smile your answer,
and mine comes with flavor

Verbi

Go into the night, past the sounds of the garden, the murmur of mice underfoot, competition's dripping skirts drying on the bushes, regret's ashes burning in the grate.

Go into the night, where only the sound of everything different can be heard, turning over like marshmallows underwater, lit by moon and shine, sparkling wonders, each one, a lovely brass ring shining in the nose of a charging bull.

I have pulled the pins out one by one, removed my toe rings, pierced myself with poppies and painted my own tears like stringed rubies in my belly. This belly will not grant me immortality, nor give me answers to soothe my fever, this cat will not avoid scratching my shoulders when he wants to feed, this ice storm will break overhead and shower down her shards of anger until everything is covered.

Blissful morning, the velvet covers of illusion, where voices are muffled by sleep. I would take your hand and dive into the pool, feeling the too-hot burn on my fair skin, peeling underneath for the black, brown and purple that live in my blood.

I hear you ancestor, I know your voice, I know your touch. You tell me it's alright to be restless, alright to be waiting for something else. You tell me to fear and live for it both. You tell me to change my name if I feel it's the only way to express who I am, so that people will see past this freckled skin and red hair, my Saxon mist that beguiles the truth, I am no more white than a cloud is substantial, I am no more your lover than I am a bird, because love is only a word they gave us once, when they made up language and sound.

Underwater you can't hear anything but the rush of blood in your ears and the incredible nearness of passion, gurgling in between your legs and out your tongue. Give me a piece of bread, a sip of wine, and the salt from your neck, hold my fingers until they turn pink and pull me with you through the vines and into the meadow, where hummingbirds die in droves and mud is amber under the moon. Give me back the moment I found myself, and leave me sore staring up at the sky.

I will never leave and I will never lie.

Gypsy

If I were not trapped
by my own making in a well
where light filtered in just enough
for shadows to press against me
in their shaded hush
reminding me perpetually
with their low rhythmic song
of a life I could have lived
if I had just been strong

your life by comparison
is in every way as wild
as the silver on the horizon
when the moon slips beneath
violet clouds and cusps
in slow formation and bows
to white flowers beneath ivy
where only moonlight finds
magic in the way you live
every moment to the end

The Corn-maker

Leave me
a moment more of this
quiet love
unspoken
to absolve belief
a mind of questions
melting her own conscience
without grace
falling
over myself to be heard
there is time yet
for change in the sky
you were born to it
turned from your journey
by the definition of my existence
making holes in the future
the razzle-dazzle of dreams

Leave me
one broken string
to follow your road
light with stars
sleeping flowers in bloom
pursing their feathered lips for a drink
of your immutable eyes

dark
beneath thought
racing like tigers in the grass
Lionheart
of gold mane and amber stare
my own
lost in water
my blood

my child

Here you are now
lying beside me
chewing my conscience
the warm salt of my youth

while your life ebbs like dust
caught in the latch of a window
out there by the cottage
of fallen corn-heads blushed with rain
imprinting your existence
surging into my body

you came with love
oh so much love

Hedgerows

Will
turning from the mirror
smudging my eye-shadow one day
rouging my lips
and smiling at
the good things about life
will
I suddenly think of you
lying in your cradle
suckling at my breast
with your tight hungry mouth
and the turning of my face
from child to mother
softer like a painting
painted underwater
will I
wonder
what you are thinking
in that blink of life
fighting over
the last time
I said goodbye

The mirror and the sea serpent

She was watching from the bed at the fat-farm,
I put on the black G-string and turned around so she could see that my buttocks were
high and firm.
I asked her how much she thought I needed to lose,
pinching nothing between thumb and forefinger and kicked the mirror,
falling into pieces.
I tore off my tights, they clung to my legs like broken cobwebs,
I bit him on the arm and inserted my fingers into his mouth
and he dragged me hard onto the pulse and we did it there,
we did it there

It was about the dance,
everything was.
You could be a man wearing a dress,
a woman wearing a dildo,
a baby wearing a moustache,
but if you gave me a drink,
a drag of your fag and a few fingers of snuff,
I would stay up all night and entertain you in purple light

If my heart could burn any faster I would probably have exploded
and become that light we see when the shore rolls back
and the sand reflects like a mirror against the blue hue of nothingness.
If you'd stayed then I might have changed everything but you left and the glow inside
burnt out,
leaving me,
turning marbles inside my mind like sand blown across glass

Weave

The shuttle taking you away was cancelled
heat in winter streaked the streets white
cats uncounted left their paws in dust
counterclockwise along the glass of cars

I wanted to be everywhere and nowhere
never to hear a telephone
or computer whir
but the death rattles of desert air
whipping the cans in unison
stillborn inside their crates
tinkering with solitude like a lizard
licking moisture from red dirt

My life is pasted on the inside of a circle
you can't read the beginning or the end
it rolls like silverfish in a bathtub
where the water is warm and woven
dragging you underneath
like rolling wool into tight balls
and watching it fall loose again
you were the moment before this one
shiny in defiance, banana skin on your feet
we skated the surface looking for whales
beached by their dreams
but there was only refuge from yesterday
bobbing in water like Christmas baubles
neglected on surf

You told me

The quiet hum of the cat, warming my lap
outside the first frost in a warm country burns the green leaves brown
a message blinks on the phone that nobody wants to retrieve
books go unread and collected in piles
your eyes wander from this
into the salt-filled air of his world
further than it seems even when you visit
where a seal pulls from the waves and follows the footsteps
blanching the shingle with quiet intrusion
where you learn Swedish to understand the motivations
behind a love you thought you'd forgotten to enact
the innocence of finding it in someone else's eyes
and the conflict of the past arguing with today's feelings
don't you know? love happens before you realize?
and nothing's wrong apart from being here
wanting this isolation, hating this isolation
needing you as I always have, and in my boat
dark against the moon
heading further out into the water
until shore cannot be found
noise is drowned
and silence in her airy wave,
sits about me like a veil
only then, in absence
in the slow drift from commonplace
with strange new things and different voices
market places comprised of empty bowls
the golden shine of a penny falling into the gutter
and mud in my toes making walking a little harder
only then, in absence
can I hope to know myself
you told me

In about 45 minutes I'm gone (or ode to leaving a job)

After 3.5 years it's come to this
I don't have anything special to wear,
I am not particularly glamorous but I type fast. Laughing loudly; "Damn boys and girls, you'll have to take me as I am."
(*exits with loud applause*)
(*turns and bows*)
(*kisses the hand of a beautiful lady and makes her blush*)
(*is chased down the street by naked women calling her name and crying pitifully*)
(*the skies open and a rainbow falls into the street, she runs up the rainbow*)

You

If I could find you out there wanting the same as me,
I'd know it, recognize it, our hands would meet, hot and shaking,
you'd kiss me for waiting, tongue salty and surprised,
the passion of knowing we're finally going to do it,
you'd put my name in yours, force the ring on my cold fingers,
put your hand on my back like you owned me,
smell my underwear and get inside my bottles of pills.

We'd present ourselves as the consummate couple,
fucking in public only to waltz in private.
I'd place the money under your pillow and leave my shoes beside your bed,
my lipstick on your collar, my scent on your thighs,
my photograph winking,
cold coffee and lilies on the table like we'd just got up and rolled over,
your child in my belly like a hawthorn blossoming.
And I'd have my green river, and you'd have your inner-peace.
So where are you? When I need you most?

Imitation of Life

My mother told me I was so impressionable
asked me whether I knew myself
who I really was
not the shadow of this
or the imitation of that
nor the fickle girl who
flicks her wrist at a lifetime
in favor of a drink with a stranger

She said
'ask yourself who you are?'
'why you must be someone else?'
'why you cannot be yourself?'
'what do you run from?'
'what inside you do you dislike?'
'what dark center recoils?'

Slipping from one to another
is like falling into black water
unable to see the surface
unable to hear yourself scream
unable to move but downward
where the air is thin
sucking out of you like wind
bubbles on the surface
can't be seen in the dark
and so you vanish without knowing
how you came to this point

Desert

In the blink of an eye
rounding the cumin road
tearing the sun from the sky
and scattering it
you come into my life
hitching your way to change
the inky oil of your hair
dirty with the journey
smelling of wild thyme
and eggs fried in animal fat
counting the stains
on your faded cords
slung like ribbons
slow moments like this
the hiss of freedom

like water in a desert
sinking faster than the eye
like a shadow in fire
in the instant you stop to listen
possibilities flickering
cards of an open deck
you pick the queen
like ripening fruit on cactus leaves
beckoning the eagle down from his flight
come taste me, know me
find the magic inside

Manger of constellations

People need to learn how to stand without falling
to the drum of every incantation
sliding over themselves in hook-eyed confusion
climbing inside to find their fit
birth canal of life an endless recycle

your mother gave you one chance to be her improvement
not to give away your soul before you knew it
or close the door when angels pound on it
lying still beneath your glittering gown
tall candles running with the oil of Isis

an onionskin of boxes interwoven
it's the way you select your battles
skin your prey and find salvation
in the christening denied us
like incense from church mice

the tailors, the storytellers, the whore-mongers
and tightrope-walkers, in their deerskin shoes
soft as butter, welts on their thighs
where the line pulls too tight
take away your authority
and the power in your pocket
and you are just another stone
picked at random and thrown
skimming the surface
catching sunlight on your back
until you plunge with the rest

what's your pleasure?
lightning on the horizon
navigating the circus of fog
driving slower with your headlights on

catching songs murmuring through the mist
and the polystyrene cup steaming
half-eaten bread sticks

roll the dice
these are the migrating moments of life

Everglades

You live in between this reality and something
driven so hard inside you the edges burn
your hands are shaking behind your brave smile
holding it together remains even in good times
a gentle incline
such is the fate of brightness
beset on the wheel of fortune
to ebb and flow like the rocket
I sent into space to find you
and bring you closer to the everglades
cool, green and untouched
by the somersaults of desire
where inside expectation's garter
we find there is not so much difference
between your explosions and my stillness
it is only the journey we choose
ending both with a wish to experience
the same thing

Damask

Jar of clay
white to keep the light inside
sharp with teeth
a milky fang by moon
gray-eyed demon you
woo me into circles

I am only one
where you go, I find myself
sleeping by the same sounds
curled in wooden cots
rocked by a warm chant
your hand on mine like imprint
underneath the soil grows life
sowing harvests and other moonlight

I am not here
more than the elemental tide
brushes the shore with thoughts
too inky to go unnoticed
the squid die in batches
staining the salt purple
sighing into the night
a chorus low and reedy

Nimble dance of spirits
this cascade of green water
ripening in my mind
like deep buried seeds
wild in their journey

I am not yours
yet, in **destiny's** caravan
sitting by the wet wood of travel

smelling of **lilies'** breath
still burnt from eating juniper leaves

You take my loss
make it into cake, crumble it
confetti over my shoulders
welding our lives
until they grow without light

I remember loving you
sealed inside my mind
the coiled copper of intention
vibrating with memory
yes

Love me like that
touch me deep and long
with the sound of deer
close-by and a creaking tree
protecting in foliage
its little acorn bride
my cusped planet shy

I am not born here
nor live in this smooth hour
for your world to capture
and imprison behind glass
stuffed with assurance

You can try to restrain
the flight of birth
bespeaking the land with blood
warm and fresh from within me

Where it lands
flowers grow into stars

rising in one voice
red with a fuzzy stem

For moments such as these
I leave behind my tongue
make your patterns on me
I have gone

Just a little treacle

I was ten when I first kissed a girl
sitting under my grandmother's apple tree
I noticed how red her cheeks were
how chapped her skin got when she went out bare-legged
I saw the woman she would become
all the creams she'd wear
fighting the likelihood of physical decline
like a butterfly fighting a bee
the sting of life not yet upon her
fragile, yet strong in an untainted paint
a quiet blue like an unripe plum
I kissed her then, once hard, once soft
when she ran away crying to her mother
I pretended I'd been dreaming of a prince
it was all just a misunderstanding
which if you think about it
sums up the majority of love
unless it comes unbidden and fresh
like spring to frost

Drowning in Tenerife

Fidgeting in the psychiatrist's chair
spinning and spinning it
making the world blurred
a little sense in confusion
do you remember the towel stained red?
falling at the crab pool, hitting rock
watching the bubbles of air as you drop
thinking you live forever
when you're young

the candle never seems to grow short
bravery seduces fear before you know it
things that scare you become funny
friends come and go like rain showers
days are measured by minutes not hours
beach stragglers, people crowding round
watching blood ooze from your head
thinking you live forever
when you're young

running away seems logical
destiny roams in her heavy skirts
pulling your curiosity to new heights
every impulse is a chocolate box
nighttime glows with exhausted promise
flesh is only flesh, only human
eventually we all collect scars
thinking you live forever
when you're drowning in Tenerife

The Deity

I fell in love with my mother
crafting her out of the hard granite
found in the woollen hills of Wales
my feet swimming in mud as I climbed
tears burning me as they froze
strange nighttime earth oozing through my toes
drying in the harsh summer sun that never
warmed enough to sunbathe
yet, in an unobserved moment
could bake the clay on your face
turn you native, lost on the elemental tide
it ran a long red line
the embryonic water mixing with earth

I built an effigy, colored with need
of you, whom I wanted years ago
lying in my bed crying for you
reaching, snatching the air with empty hope
wishing in tongues of childhood
for your return
a thin white door
seeing the chink of light blink on
grow larger against the blue swirls of the carpet
white linoleum underneath
reminding me of a sea opening
your tanned arm on the door knob
your voice that I heard singing in madness

in despair you sang to me before I was born
reciting ways of coping, lapsing into stages
where you could unravel me and dance alone
gathering my attempts at love like twine
and feeding fish with the leftovers
had you wanted me then?

had I been just a weight in your belly?
a life without armor asking for protection
not a carbon of you, somehow unrecognized
growing heavier and more demanding
like the picture books showed me
a quiet 'C' in-utero

Therapist # 2

I combed my hair until it sat
hiding the scar
turned the collar up on my shirt
and folded my legs
to face slightly away
as I leaned in
listening to your heart
beating like a Moroccan pipe
against a dark quiet night
'what?' you asked
dry-mouthed and timid
your eyes remind me of lamps
burning with a precious fuel
'where have I been?' you ask
'you've been traveling' I say
turning my hands in my lap
examining the moles that have grown
in-love with the sun
a little endearment
a little perfume in the carpet
and as you stretch I add;
'we're going to stop here
stay for a while
and see if anything glows
in the darkness

Memory

You sat on the edge of the bed
oppressing the room with good intentions
laid mute for the first time
since you began expanding your horizons
if I could have understood
you'd have told me what it was like
living in a tenement world
walking to school with a satchel
crossed over your chest to ward off
the paving stone demons

how even now
you'd sell everything
just to escape the cool indifference of
your mother's midday sherry
lost on denial's kind sail
she closed your door at night
you could hear her sigh on the other side
clutching your dreams to you in the darkness
watching out, the window lights go out
one by one
knowing the door would open
you would not be alone to dream
he taught you seven languages
the names of every port-town he'd visited

reminded you to study hard and make him proud
breath of figs and cigars and Egyptian aftershave
you closed your eyes and thought of Conrad novels
climbing into jungles and flying over tree tops
lost in cultures that talked to you
murmuring possibilities into adulthood

on the same bed you pack your life

into a little bag hardly large enough
your eyes turn to me
the same eyes that stared out of the window
twenty years before
I breathe in and let you know
it's all right to leave

I intend to follow
if not now, then soon
and you smile a terrible smile
as if this was the first time
love let you free

For my Mother

Fame

Don't feel sorry for me
I am the ant-turned-butterfly
roaming in plastic
caught by my vision
this world
just enough madness for
another hot flush

Don't feel sorry for me
I am the girl who takes her glasses off to see
walking barefoot on glass
wearing wool in the summer
and nothing in the rain
just enough madness for
real clarity

Don't feel sorry for me
I am here when you are there
nesting in emptiness
the sounds of my own
hardship and pity
playing poker in the back room
just enough madness for
another shot at fame

Mine

In 1992 everything happened
I walked into a lake
killed my child
watched grandmother die
struck grandfather for lying
jets flew over us as the earth turned gray
we fucked in the grass in the middle of the day
I cried so hard the sound stayed inside
it was never enough to say I had a bad year
I changed inside like brandy
sliding in your glass like warm oil
OUT went hope. IN came defeat
she rolled me into a ball and cut off my feet
I shot like a firework down the hill
gathering speed, gathering weeds.

Underwater you can't breathe unless you stop
thinking about things that don't change
the beating of your heart
the purr of sex in your ear
the empty bed that smells of love
growing cold year by year
grief is like an apple
wormed from inside out
grief is a heart washed for dinner
cooling on the table
slowing, slowing, pulse mine
listen to another tune
snort another line
and dance with me lover
to the melancholy hop of life
a jig between the sheets
a bloodied towel in the trash
reminding me, vivid scarlet

of all the things I lost
all the things I gained
from the emergence of a woman
from a year of living pain

Relation

I met a man on the road to hell
he said he was turned right
because his left hand betrayed him
marked with the devil
so he painted it red to remind him
which way to avoid

I met a man on the road to hell
he said I was a prick-teasing bitch
not worth dying for or writing about
but enough to get under his skin
and leave a sting
the size of a quarter

I met a man on the road to hell
he wanted to drink my blood
and part my thighs
to expose the bits of me I had left
feast on me he said, then
let life feast on you

I met a man on the road to hell
and thought with my big plans
I could save him too
only he didn't want saving
he wanted to take me down
shoot me between the eyes and leave me
spread in a fork to show him the way

A little death

The woman that dies of AIDS
will not have a new dress this year
or bandages for her scars
or milk for her dying baby
or live husband for burying
when she dies
the wood on her coffin will be the cheapest
perhaps the ground too inviting
she will leap
from her death to the earth
and turn ochre with the setting sun

Cheese Plate

Time to turn the tape over
listen to another mind
aside my own
stumbling with street names
fornicating with feathered dress
shaking hands and wide mouth
expectant of some offered delight
white paint on my soles
purple under my tongue
where the pill has lain
the crows in the trees
that bruised color of winter
watching me tie my shoes
pick the scab on my elbow and
marvel at bones protruding
youth in absence
an unopened package of lychees
turning into fermented perfume
you left them behind as payment
parting my thighs with promises
of beaches and t-shirts
seeing my eyes underwater
watching you opening me
like a can of peas
green and new

Lint

I had a sister once
sitting at the top of the stairs in Ealing Broadway
her dark feet and my teeth gleaming
up late, past the mandala hour
where all things circular
remind us of mirrors
afloat on the Thames
the Seine
the little patch of wet
at the foot of the bed
soaking up my tears
leaving behind the dried and salted fears
like miniature shards of glass
caught under your skin
glitter
white rain
silence again
she turned to me her mouth pomegranate red
kissed me as someone loved
rubbed her velvet dress against my hair
making it shine in the darkness
leaving a trace of childhood
lint

Coins for a Funeral

He is a new zephyr
breathing fire upon lilies until they melt
waxed by violence for fast paced consideration
falling pearls back to the seabed
invisible, as once I was
strewn in your arms for slaughter
silver piece in my mouth
hard to the bite, sucking on metal
worth less, more than life
blooming on cusps of circular bonfires
lighting skies with savage memory
your hands pulling me under the water
where static weeds grow lithe fingers
entering me in green vision
I let go of the borders, they blurred
glasses crushed into diamonds
where moon winks heavily at transgression
joins the circles that compound begotten earth
where did you bury my heart?
which tree holds my blood?
do the leaves that unfurl like dancers
know these names as well?
silence that hangs in unison
painted stiff and yoked
dress a bloody reminder
all things spilt
all things best remedied
beneath buried attempt

Part Deux

You, the silent china owl
screaming white noise into the night
a corridor of doors
closed too tight

You, the pinching fingers in dark
pulling me tenderly, pulling me apart
a basket of worms
writhing for soil
as the sun bakes them
one
by
one

You, the sharp silhouette
pulling my head back
forcing my mouth
exploring my nightmares
with a torch and rope

You, mama, momma, mia, me
something of the same
a little this, a little that
petite accidents
sweet, then sour, then..
violently snapped back
bloody

Similarity

I know your movements as my own
a shadow, brightness, a telltale memoir
eclipsing the sun, bemusing the birds
falling from the trees like splinters on our spilt blood

our dance around in heavy gypsy skirts
and lowered eyes painted black and unseeing
is as slow as the hesitant beating of midnight's heart
rising out of the clouds like a Spanish virgin

I know your movements as my own
where saffron grows thick and yellow on memory
obscuring the white rays of midday sun that relentless
try to bleach our history to muted chalk

Hazel Eyed Sex

Direct your climax into the sheets
made wet in motion
laughter dries underneath
this finger-fucked battery
vibrating good intentions and dirty children
raised in the heat of regret
get it over with
if that's your thing to
rip and thrust
eat the living out
leave the dead
for recycling
and afterthought

All Things

All things
as the butterfly nears her end
her dance ever frantic
catching colors against leaves
burnished shyly
another flower breaks
the soft soil
where sun falls like
rain infused light
all things then
seem eternal

Sweet Silent Static

Is there a desert far enough
to reach no rain?
tears turn to dust
rather than feel again
where pain turns inward
like the conch, the shell, the lizard skin, the blackness within
so deeply like nitrite forcing life
from things limp and unwilling to confide
their unsaid agonies to final death
is defeat when you feel nothing?
where the greatest pain is just a splinter
on the circular deception of a big wheel
lolling its tongue at the moon?
if being alone hurts then being deceived
is the dance on top of knives
sharpened for the wit of a storm
and merciless in their precise cuts
all tiny and unnoticeable
enough to build a river of blood
enough to remove the want for a tongue
you smiled that great big smile that
caught me forever grinning back in love
and it was the abyss we both mirrored
shattering and rebuilding like nightmares
cycling on repeat
sweet silent static

Goodbye & Hello

Sunday's burnt eggs lie like weeping circles of yellow emotion in bright grass
reminding me of the lizard eaten, half dying, dragging its remainder to the light
as if light scores us pure and saved, like diving into cool water and breathing no more
scalding air and voices, begging for our attention like red ants at dusk

I want no more welts, no more advertisements for 'happy career roommate'
no more of this expected bloated world bursting on the seams of another pregnant
moment

I want the crying red of sunsets, muted by silence deeper than canyon
I want the brush of your hands in mine, the echo of rivers unseen, washing our sin
I want the abandon of falling stars lighting the cactus flowers and shape shifters with
unearthly silver like it was when hope was only a child and she expected rabbits on her
window at Easter and cruelty to be a character in a book, not the pinch of maddening
tucking her in at night

Here where even air beats a glowing drum, the flicker of poison runs thinner
reminds me not of scars now corseted in years, the bleat of betterment beguiling
memory

We dance under pungent flowers where darkness looks to be on fire with the moon
and all things happy sway like urgent pollen catching the limber wind to faraway

Tigers not daughters

You and I, whether wanting it or not
are pierced by the same wound, the same blood
rooted and buried deep with green fingers
when the sun climbs high and swallows burst their songs
far above tall trees dazzling with new shoots
when sprinklers turn on and make their hum and hiss
we emerge from the earth like overnight weeds
planted haphazardly and left to forage life
a poppy on the side of the road able to grow toward the light
caught between rocks and litter with no soil for sustaining
beautiful against the angry roar of passing cars
we are tigers, not daughters

We are built of stalagmites and stalactites
glittering in caves filled with echoes
for all the sadness there is merriment only we understand
when after dark we daub ourselves with greasepaint
and run through the lawns in pursuit of each other
I run to you, you run to me, we run from the absorbing ache
of misunderstanding, playing tricks in the grass
where cats roam unmolested like tigers
we live also in that twilight, catching moths and fireflies
leaving no trail, because we do not want to be found
we are tigers, not daughters

"Tigers not daughters,"
Taken from King Lear, by William Shakespeare.

Today's Observation

Muhammad Ali's training camp is for sale on EBay
I'd rather buy some Yohji Yamamoto Adidas slippers
or a crepe de chine nightgown from the 1940s
because I just saw Bette Davis in Dead Ringer
curled in a divan with satin gloves up to her elbows
and I feel like being crazy behind a veil with a Great Dane at my heel
though for today I'll content with Thai green curry and reality TV show
but I know there's something wrong with a life that doesn't glow
could it be that in rushing life, we're all becoming slow mo?

Chick-a-Flicker

Grow up
there was a time for being angry
now be smart
take courses, get qualified, get a job
go conquer the world
leave anger behind at the door
where it starts

there's a time for anger
its hand holds youth not age
age is a place of sensibility and stillness
listen to the growth of your 401k
potted plants on your window
the cat's mottled craw as he cleans his genitals

be glad for your well-compensated job
you got by going to the right school
sucking the right cock
kissing the right door to open to the next and the next and the next
until all doors are flung
gaping and inviting

you take the world by the proverbial balls
shove them high and dance in red heels on a spinning globe
spitting teeth and infamy like goblets of mead

squeeze out a kid
just so you can say
ten years down the road
want to see my photos?
a passing fear of loneliness
assuaged
by the neglect you'll fester like starving a lover
makes him hungrier

your child
without knowing why
will love you more than you'll ever care
for your acquisitions, historical nonce, collection of vibrators

and when at 45 you nick yourself shaving
you'll wonder what drips from your legs
whether it's possible you still bleed
given all inside is long dead
and wrapped up in corporate cling-film
ready to be processed

you tell people now
grow up
get a move on
lose yourself
before you give another moment's thought
to anything besides what you were taught
to buckle down, strap in place, wear with pride
the starched suits, the shiny briefcase
girl-scout prim

you tell people now
grow up
before out of the corner of every moment
the caustic laugh, the speculative glance
the hours spent stirring lifeless things
an empty dance
leaking
truths
like lemon rind
acidic
bitter on the tongue
rolling along
for no one to find

The night I turned 16

Time gathers her skirts a little faster
each year turning
the roses that were nimble buds
fall open as a curtsey
shedding their now smudged petals
in maddening pathways of color
such is the turning from late summer
still warming the garden stones
hearing crickets murmuring below and
fish sunning themselves on the water's edge
here I am
walking in the high grass toward your house
a funny feeling of destiny gurgling in my stomach
like sour lemonade and popping candy mixed into fireworks
lit just for you on the night I turned 16

The copper wedding dress

I have my dress, a crescent violet
silken and half transparent wing
lying on the back of a hotel chair
reflecting prisms on the floor
I look at my feet
flat and broad from dancing
ugly toes with crooked points
cool on the wooden floor, feeling
the heartbeat of trees under my skin
one, two, three silver voices
calling me to the forest again
'marry me there' I call out
falling through the burnished leaves
into the lake, into moist earth
gentle ugliness enveloping
cleansing my pretense
washing from me the chalky smell
of living above

here, my heart beats slower
more in tune with you
my eyes are shadowed with tulips
showered in lightless dew
warmed by burnished crystal
by the light of love's fire

foxes red and brown in a lair
deer with their oval whispering eyes
lambs milky and unsteady on their feet
wolves sharpening their wit against me
diving with the birds who live underground
falling to earth's circle
overhead the bower of roses blush
we eat the copper wedding cake

piece by piece
drink dandelion tea by the stars
first you, then me

Pursuing Different Tracks

A published writer advised
"Don't write about yourself,
you sound like a teenager crying over spilt milk.
Write observations, things outside of you,
or poetry becomes selfish and inward,
and nobody wants to hear a person's thoughts anymore.
The formula, it's all in the formula.
You get it right, you have it, you sell it."
She's even in bookstores that don't have poetry sections
she's doing-poetry-on-tour,
inspiring fledgling poets, who
write about things outside themselves,
in neat obedient mixed-shake-formula.
Sometimes at night, when trains go by,
I think about what she said.
If I can see in the dark
I walk outside and look up at the sky,
bigger than me, a thing outside myself
and next time I write
"I saw the moon, it made me think of sadness, it made me
remember things inside myself and they rolled over like mice in a wheel straining for speed."
I think owing to this,
my books won't have pretty covers
won't move a generation
the moon will continue to reflect thoughts inside to without
and that's just how it is
when trains wake you at night
pursuing different tracks

A Jar for the jarring

How I felt saying goodbye
Playing the piano
before the dust jacket is replaced
the shutters drawn
and we leave
our house
for winter

Infidelity

Is like a drink un-drunk
left in the sink
flow down
steel against sentiment
I hear a bird sing
in the lightness
and that song was sad
breaking against
glass
shattering
against me

Send me with you

You take me as I am
that bird with feathered intent
brush-strokes of apricot embers
rubbed on your hands in mine
listening to LPs on a new stereo
as if then was now and now is then
send me with you
through time
the moment we met, past and long before
drawing circles in our imagination
a song lasts long after the needle
makes a soft hum
shifting like laughter
through silver trees

Merry-Go-Round

How bright darkness is,
when lit with sparklers in woollen fingers,
measured against the moon acting with
Baskervilles through veiled cloud play
the tips of your red skirts,
rushing colors, a merry-go-round,
as laughter permeates silence,
punctuated breaths of wind, surrounding reality,
whipping away our now orphan scarves,
some quickly, flipping cat tails, electric in air,
where will they land?
where will we be when you stop turning?
and time ticking beckons us again to perfunctory
and plain, muddy tracks blurred with insight,
washing away night's colors,
like crayons in rain

Lark

Grief is a filament, dusk, dust, dimly pirouetting
your ash my fire your water my earth
all is covered by empty words laid down over birth
hand them off to the crows before the tree grows
let them find other silver ways than your cruelty sharp displayed
free now in mixing amber and blue
create color from grey, find flight before fools crowd and spin
turning all sense into a mystery thing

I want with you to go

This is not yours to keep
leave hope for fools who seek to sleep
all around stars swallow darkness whole
refusing pitch as light burns through years
will you climb through space's faring soul
and rescue me from this interminable unknown?
I don't recognize my place in the play
all is unfamiliar and at odds with what's safe
there's no end to an elongated day of thought
ending with no more, no less, just naught
if somehow you'd find me now,
taking my eagerness into the clouds
I'd re-learn to believe, I'd gather fragments of my heart
plaster them back stronger, this time to last
where stars glow, night cannot swallow whole
that aching place where flayed ribbons fly
I'd like to remember dancing again
I'd like to touch my toes
it's not enough to miss this
I want with you to go

Who leaves behind

Who
Leaves behind
Promises like confetti
Scattered
My arms ache
An empty place between
Where you were
Folded close to my heart
Now
Windows flung carelessly
Raw sea breezes and mocking
Wielding birds higher than sight
Feet raw with sand
Nothing else
Even night cusps against moon
Trying not to disturb
A hush fallen on this place
Since you took the words
Left hollow shells
Paving roads in water
Leading only deeper
Where nobody returns whole
As if never, touch or sound
Existed in more than memory
As fine as dried salt
Caught on the hem of everything
Leaching a little color
With each rinse

Red felt

Your eyes ache from staring too brightly
All the missing stitches on holly go lightly
Rampant mirth cavorts in red letter eat
Finish your spinach or kiss your betters
Rummaging for the right color eyeball
With guts that raw you don't have to fall
Hold me up, I mislaid my bones
Too fast, too thickly spoken out loud
What of this plunge a birth in reverse
From eclipses come brightly to darkness
I had a tongue once with silvered glib
Your joy, your merriment, now leaves me stiff
Less than a well-caught gown, this reversible puppet
One side red caped, the other, wolf
I fold myself inside out and scream
No sound penetrates further than your own shroud

Were I born and you not

Were I born and you not
Translation from lost to naught
What steps taken without you
To sinking water's empty vacuum
You give me words and measure
I climb a syllable in slowly leisure
Without in my frame a glance
Of furtive smile winking
The moon would not glow bright enough
To set me right in this long night
Without you by my side
Other things remain unthinking
You raise the blind you quench the light
You bring me sight and dream
In your long glance and child's cheek
All else is Ink's dove to waste
Turning from color in water opaque

Clay

All source in one light
As clay rising from river's pull can
Seem smooth in a fickle marvel
What of these shapes
Fathomed from water lying heavy
On a bed of wriggling ideas
Teeming with same dreams
What are hands formed from
Being held underwater in fits
Of rising swells and crying falls
A river you call it, a world into more
Where birds molded of earth given life
Strike into newborn skies leaving
Excited plumes of interrupted sunset
For us to follow, once we reach
Each other's form, breathing
As one stream, leaving wet for air
Lighter than anything except the fragile
Moment our clay hearts find their beat

Hear the Steps

Hear the steps, light in tread, heavy intent
Hear the child, cries her first, as you cry yourself
All the way down to darkness's keep
Where light fades in favor of silencing dusk
Clouding truth from fancy in drifting part
Once I could follow dancing behind in smiles
Now I hang myself heavy, and trail in guise
Nothing, nothing but the sound of rain hides
That toxic, that lonely, that ever-there shame
It wears me as a red skirt wears dancing in waves
The bird flying higher than rest, reaching clouds
Reaching a place of no blame

Destiny

I come from a world of push and pull
the stones thrown never killed
like eels they wormed inside my gut
eating my strength and leaving empty knots
they tied me down, you held me up
like a puppet I played to a tuneless plot
nobody not even myself knew why
these singular arrows decide to fly
hitting one by one their target, my heart
bleeding and wrought in pain and dark
all I ever wanted was to belong to you
to hold hands and feel, without fear it was true
something given never to be taken
I could know I had finally awakened
it would all come right, all feel meant to be
like the first time I saw you, and you saw me